Stickball, Streetcars And Saturday Matinees

Illustrated Memories by Cliff Wirth

REMINISCE BOOKS

Editor: Mike Martin
Assistant Editors: Kristine Krueger, Mike Beno, Henry de Fiebre
Art Director: Maribeth Greinke
Art Associate: Gail Engeldahl
Production Assistants: Ellen Lloyd, Judy Pope
Publisher: Roy J. Reiman

© 1995, Cliff Wirth
Reiman Publications, L.P.
5400 S. 60th St., Greendale WI 53129

International Standard Book Number: 0-89821-151-4
Library of Congress Catalog Number: 95-69028
All rights reserved. Printed in U.S.A.

For additional copies of this book or information on other books, write: Reminisce Books, P.O. Box 990, Greendale WI 53129. **Credit card orders call toll-free 1-800/558-1013.**

Introduction

By Cliff Wirth

AS I LOOK BACK on my Depression-era childhood, it always amazes me how much *fun* we had. Although money was not plentiful, my memories of those days are happy ones.

That's why I am delighted to share these memories in the color illustrations that follow. Not many people get the opportunity to so thoroughly re-experience the pleasures of their childhood.

For me, those wonderful growing-up years centered around an old two-story frame house at 110 Lexington Avenue in Bayonne, New Jersey. That's where my sister, Doris, my two older brothers, Donald and Fred ("Buddy" and "Fritzie"), and I were raised.

I was a year old when my mother died in 1928. With four kids under age 10, Dad was forced to move us from Pittsburgh to Bayonne so we could be with our grandparents. Dad's business required him to be away from home a lot, so Grandma and Grandpa pretty much took over the job of raising us.

Even though they'd already raised six children of their own, they gladly took on the chore of raising four more young kids. I

DOWNHILL THRILLS. Although Cliff and his brothers, "Buddy" and "Fritzie", often had to "triple up" on their Flexible Flyer, it didn't dampen their enthusiasm one bit.

doubt Grandma and Grandpa thought they were doing anything special by taking us in…back then, people in trouble turned to their families.

As we grew up, Grandpa and

"We had a sense of community that seems to be lost today…"

Grandma gave us all the attention and love any kids could have asked for. Along the way, assorted aunts, uncles and cousins helped make life great for us, too.

Back then, Bayonne was a blue-collar town of roughly 100,000 souls situated at the southern end of a peninsula on the "Jersey side" of New York Bay (New York City was directly across the bay to our east).

Some of the biggest local employers in those days were the oil refineries and naval shipyards.

Industrial Town Hard Hit

Like similar industrial cities all across the country, Bayonne was hit hard by the Depression, and it deepened soon after we arrived there. But we kids were relatively unaware of the nation's economic problems.

Everyone in our neighborhood was in the same boat, so there was no stigma attached to not having money. In a way, it brought us all closer together. Besides, most of the fun things we did cost little or nothing.

Our earnings from collecting soda bottle deposits enabled us to cheer cowboy heroes like Hoot Gibson on Saturday afternoons at the Plaza, or buy the latest Green Lantern or Captain Marvel comic book down at Blanco's grocery store.

Money we got by selling "junk" to the junkman financed purchases of "Rockwoods" (remember those tasty little chocolate candies?), jawbreakers and charlotte russes…all of the really important things in life.

We played stickball and boxball in the street, and baseball and football in nearby vacant fields. In winter, my brothers and I piled on our Flexible Flyers and sledded down the Third Street hill.

Enjoyed "Water Sports"

During summer, we'd go swimming, fishing or crabbing in the Kill Van Kull (the narrow body of water that separated Bayonne from Staten Island just to the south).

We rode excursion boats to Rye Beach and ferryboats to Staten Island, and spent many a happy hour playing "cops and robbers" in my Uncle Clem's junkyard.

In the evenings, we (and just about everyone else who had access to a radio in Bayonne) listened to *The Shadow*; *Jack Armstrong, the All-American Boy*; *One Man's Family*; the *Lux Radio Theatre*; *Jack Benny*; and *Bob Hope*.

The whole neighborhood discussed these programs often, and had a sense of community that seems to have been lost in today's world.

Believe me, it was a lot harder for kids to get in serious trouble when everyone in the neighborhood knew you. Our local priest, Father Doyle, patrolled the streets after 8 p.m., making sure children were at home like they were supposed to be. If he "collared" you, he'd drag you home to face your parents' wrath.

Father Doyle had the uncanny ability to appear out of nowhere—I'll never forget the night he scared the living daylights out of me down on Lord Avenue!

Kids Respected Authority

Since my grandfather was a retired police officer, it seemed like there was always somebody around who knew we were Edward Wirth's grandkids.

If you did get caught doing something wrong, you might get a "boot in the pants", but you probably expected it and weren't eager to make an issue of it (for fear your parents would hear about it and then you'd *really* be in trouble).

Back then, holidays were celebrated with a lot of verve. I fondly recall fancy parades, firecrackers and

fireworks on Independence Day.

At the big Memorial Day observance held near the monument on Fifth Street, you can bet I was one of the kids who raced to pick up spent shells from the rifle salute honoring fallen World War I veterans.

In the illustrations that follow, you'll see many old-time scenes like that, and a lot of names will keep on popping up as the memories weave through these pages. All of these people were friends, relatives or acquaintances when I was growing up in the late '30s and early '40s.

My grandfather (I called him "Pop") was a no-nonsense man whose strength helped hold our family together.

Grandpa Never Drove

The son of an immigrant German baker, he was born the year Lincoln was shot, spent almost his entire life in Bayonne and never had a driver's license. Grandpa had a little difficulty adapting to the telephone—he'd always shout into the receiver, thinking that someone so far away couldn't hear him.

My Grandma Nora watched over us like a mother hen. She darned our socks, made the best vegetable soup imaginable and must have said thousands of rosaries on our behalf.

One of my best friends was Butch Barnes. A fine stickball player, ♂→

he was our neighborhood's best athlete. It's strange to think that our friendship began with a fist fight, but it did. (I lost, which *wasn't* so strange.)

My cousin Don Titus was a year younger than me and lived five or six blocks away. He spent an awful lot of time at our house and shared in many escapades.

Uncle Clem and Aunt Eleanor were my dad's brother and sister. They were dear people who were always there when anyone in the family needed them. There must have been hundreds of occasions when they administered help, scoldings or laughter, as needed.

"Aunt El" loved to "play the numbers". I'll never forget the time she asked me to pick some numbers for her. I did, but for some reason she decided to reverse the order I'd given her. Of course, the numbers I originally gave her were the ones that came in!

Boys Admired Boilermaker

Uncle Clem was a cigar-chomping hero with a heart of gold. All the guys in the neighborhood ad-

mired him. A real handyman, he worked as a boilermaker and ran his own junkyard. Uncle Clem was the first person you went to if you were in trouble…or needed a nickel.

Captain Bunny (yes, that was his real name) was a friend of my grandfather's who ran the "Avenue C" ferry over to Staten Island. I'll never forget the time the guys and I were riding the ferry, and I bet one of them that Captain Bunny wouldn't be able to dock the ferry on the first try.

I was certain I'd win because the current was tricky, and it appeared

to be carrying us well past the ferry slip. But then, at the last possible moment, Captain Bunny revved the engines and brought us in as pretty as you please. What a touch at the helm!

Jerry Blanco ran the corner grocery store at Fourth Street and Lexington, two doors down from where we lived. That same store had a pinball machine in back— which one day gave me the electric shock of my life. I was trying to "rig" the machine at the time, so I guess I deserved it.

Georgie Halagowski was a next-door neighbor and good friend

SPARKS AND SPLASHES. Georgie Halagowski, Cliff's neighbor, was always ready for fun—whether that meant jumping into the Kill Van Kull or watching Uncle Clem weld in his junkyard.

One more reflection on those innocent days—it seems to me that my friends and I ran *everywhere*...to school, to the streetcar, to the store, to the ball field and, at the end of the day, back home.

It was as if life was full of possibilities and we *couldn't wait* to get to wherever we were going. After all, fun wasn't found in a pocketful of money or material things, fun was wherever you found it ...and we didn't want to miss any of it.

Right now, though, I'd like to invite you to relax and savor the memories in this book at a much more leisurely pace.

I sincerely hope these illustrations—and the adventures and anecdotes that go with them—will spark memories of similar antics for those of you who remember a time when city neighborhoods were a great place for a kid to grow up.

GRANDMA'S SOUP WAS GREAT. Few fragrances were more heavenly than the aroma of Grandma's homemade vegetable soup simmering away on top of the stove. Cliff and his three siblings were the second "brood" she'd raised, but Cliff doesn't recall ever hearing her complain.

who shared in most of our adventures. He was usually available for any kind of boyhood mischief we might be contemplating, from sneaking onto the Coney Island excursion boat to diving off the pilings into the Kill Van Kull.

They Were Superman Fans

Georgie was "working" with me on the day we got so involved in an art project (chalking Superman on the street) that a slow-moving car backed right into us.

Speaking of art, I'd like to apologize for any artistic license this "old ink slinger" might have taken in rendering these scenes. In dusting off memories that are

over 50 years old, it's possible that some of the people I recall so fondly may have been inadvertently placed at or in a wrong scene.

So, to all my old friends, I'd just like to say: If you weren't actually where I've placed you, I sincerely wish you were—it probably would've been even more fun!

A TART TREAT. Grandpa was an accomplished gardener. In that garden was pucker-powering rhubarb.

The Super Salesman Comes to Visit

SPRING AND FALL were the door-to-door sales seasons in our neighborhood, and the salesman I remember most is the Fuller Brush Man. He looked so much like Ronald Coleman that, for a while, I really thought he *was* that actor.

"Is your mother home?" he'd ask when I answered the door. "Boy, I'll bet you can really slam those home runs!" he'd quickly add, reaching into his pocket and handing me a piece of bubble gum.

I'd mumble something inane, thank him for the gum, then shout, "Hey, Grandma! The Fuller Brush Man's here!"

When Grandma appeared, the salesman would remove his hat and deftly swing his huge sample case into the house. The two of them would walk together into the kitchen.

On the way, he'd launch into a fascinating warm-up speech...full of laughs, neighborhood gossip and information about exciting new products.

Grandma would take a seat at the kitchen table, as regal as Queen Victoria. Popping open his case, Ronald Coleman would present her with a new calendar, a pot holder or maybe a washcloth.

She was eating out of his hand already...but I really knew he had her when I heard this exchange.

"Cliff," she sternly addressed me, "what did I tell you about bubble gum?"

Smiling broadly, Ronald Coleman rushed to my defense, saying, "Everything's fine, ma'am. I gave him that gum...it's a new dentist-approved brand."

Grandma's stern look softened and she remarked, "Well, I guess it's all right, then."

That Fuller Brush Man's specialty was charm, and his brushes were good, too. At least, that's what Grandma said—Grandpa's only comment was, "That fella sure has the gift of gab."

Trapped in a Box Canyon!

"FROM OUT OF THE PAST come the thundering hoofbeats of the great horse 'Silver'," the radio announcer cried. "The Lone Ranger rides again!"

That was stirring stuff at our house. Grandpa would light his pipe and put down the *Bayonne Times*. Grandma would pause from reading the *Ladies Home Journal* or darning socks to grumble about outlaw Butch Cavendish ("that devil").

From the hoofbeats of Silver and 'Scout' all the way through to the show's familiar sign-off with the stirring William Tell Overture, *The Lone Ranger* held our family's undivided attention.

I loved the sound of ricocheting bullets (which my talented cousin could mimic perfectly). But my favorite sound of all was the thunderous echo of Silver's hooves as he galloped over a wooden bridge.

After the program, we kids would say our prayers, then head upstairs to our bedrooms...where unexplained noises in the attic were sure to make us think Butch Cavendish and his gang were coming to get us.

Corner Store Was Comic Book Heaven

EVERY NEIGHBORHOOD in Bayonne had a few popular spots where kids would gather to "hang out". We'd often go to a corner store on Fifth and Lord for sodas, candy and to catch up on the latest comic books.

These colorful adventure books cost a dime. That posed a problem, since those of us lucky enough to even have allowances could count on a nickel a week. But we came up with a way to read the latest comics without buying them.

The store owner allowed prospective customers only a few short glances at a comic book. After that, we'd be politely reminded to "either buy it or put it back". We'd meekly put the book down and leave the store.

But we did get enough time to read a couple of pages. So, later that day, another of us would enter the store and read two more pages. This would go on with different guys until the book was done. Then we'd get together and tell each other the whole story.

Unfortunately, our little ruse was eventually discovered. After that, the comics were displayed behind the counter and you had to ask to look. It just wasn't the same!

'Rags, Paper, Copper, Brass!'

CLANGING COWBELLS and the clip-clop of a horse's hooves on pavement announced the arrival of the junkman. Rain or shine, he showed up every Saturday morning.

"Rags, paper, copper, brass!" he'd shout from atop his old wagon, as dozens of enterprising little businessmen and businesswomen scrambled into action, each pulling a wagonful of wares to sell.

Since we were growing up in a heavy-industrial town, we had little trouble scavenging scrap metal.

I remember that it took about an hour to burn the insulation off a good-sized clump of copper wire my friends and I found days earlier. The junkman would only weigh and pay for pure metal. That made a hunk of solid brass a real find.

While I waited in line with fellow scavengers who helped me fill my wagon, visions of ice cream sodas and Saturday matinees danced in my head.

After weighing our wares on his rusty old scale, the junkman would reach into his coat, pull out his money bag and pay us.

We'd split the proceeds and walk away happily with a handful of change as the junkman and his old "hay burner" clip-clopped their way to the next neighborhood.

No Doorbells Needed in Our Neighborhood

I DON'T RECALL a kid in our neighborhood ever using a doorbell. We all had great lungs, though—after a while, you could tell who was calling for you just by the way they hollered your name.

"Hey, Cliffie!" meant either Georgie Halagowski or Tom Gibbons was looking for me. A shrill whistle and a "Yoo, Cliff!" was usually Butch Barnes. If the "Cliff!" had a little lilt at the end, I knew Joe Rifino was waiting outside for me.

But the most memorable call of all came from a little kid who lived over on Fourth Street and had trouble pronouncing our names. In a high loud voice, he'd yell, "Fishie, Tickey and Ti!" 'looking for Fritzie (my brother), Cliffie (me) and Don Titus (my cousin). That call became famous in our neighborhood and we still chuckle about it today.

I remember one afternoon I went over to Charlie Davis' house around suppertime. "Hey, Chuckie!" I called out. In a few moments, my friend came to the door with a piece of bread in his hand. Then Mrs. Davis wanted to know if I'd eaten.

When I told her I had, she asked if I was still hungry. "A little bit, I guess," I answered.

"Well then, why don't you come in and have a piece of the peach pie I just made?" she asked.

"Okay," I said as I casually ambled into the kitchen.

This conversation wasn't quite as innocent as it sounds. Earlier that afternoon, I'd been in the Davis' backyard and spotted that mouth-watering pie cooling on the windowsill.

Hey, when opportunity knocks, you have to make yourself available!

Picture Day Was a Real Pony Show

PICTURE DAY on Hobart Avenue was always a big deal for us kids.

Followed by a crowd of curious youngsters, the friendly traveling photographer would set up shop in our neighborhood. He'd adjust his camera and tripod, pose his pony "just so" and begin shooting away.

The pony didn't exactly compare with the Lone Ranger's "Silver", and the flashy 10-gallon hat was stuffed with newspaper so it wouldn't fall down over our ears. But this was as close to the Old West as any of us New Jersey kids were likely to get.

When my turn came, I was excited, because I'd never been on a horse before. Swinging up into the saddle, I noticed it was appropriately equipped with a real lariat around the saddle horn!

It was all mighty Western-looking, but I found it hard to pose like a steely-eyed lawman with my friends making cracks like, "Shouldn't you be sitting sidesaddle?" or "How about a song, Roy?"

Later, when the developed photograph arrived at the house, it earned a place of honor on the mantel, remaining there for a few months before being relegated to the family photo album.

Trip for a Trim Was a Big Deal

OUR TRIPS to the barbershop on Orient and Silver Streets became more frequent after we entered high school and started noticing the opposite sex. Until then, those trips were reserved for the beginning of school, Christmas, Easter and the start of summer vacation.

The two amiable barbers who did the actual shearing seemed to have special haircuts designed for each occasion. The Christmas and Easter trims, for example, were things of beauty. We'd walk around for at least a day afterward trying to keep each hair in place. The effect I believe they were after was a slick "George Raft look" with shiny hair and neck well-powdered.

On the day school started in September, everyone in the neighborhood looked like a movie star (the boys with their slicked-down hair and the girls with their assorted locks and hairdos). But by the end of the day, the hair of us male students was somehow restored to its natural look…i.e., completely unkempt.

Our summer haircuts were not quite "Sing Sing" or "Alcatraz", but they were close. We called them brush cuts, and it wasn't until I reached high school that I went to an actual barber for one.

Before then, Uncle Clem did the honors between greasing a wheel in his garage or welding something or other in his junkyard. His technique was utilitarian in the extreme. And, if you complained about the bare spots when he was done, his only comment would be, "Well, it'll grow back" or "You must have pulled away at the wrong time."

By the time I entered high school, I was more than happy to have at last reached official "barbershop" age.

Clapping Erasers Was Dusty Fun

I DOUBT that our eraser clapping had much of an effect on the ozone layer, but I do recall some furious white dust storms that developed along Storey Court and Fourth Street whenever the seventh-grade clappers tried to outdo the eighth-grade clappers.

There was an art to clapping erasers...it was far more than just slapping them together. The trick was not how hard you banged them together, it was how quickly you pulled them apart.

Sometimes we'd get creative and bang the erasers on the school wall, but the janitors frowned on this method.

On several occasions, our classroom chore would actually turn into a war, with erasers flying through the air and pandemonium breaking out. This usually resulted in the combatants being kept after school—but sometimes it was worth it.

My classmate John McCuster was an eraser-clapping legend because he could slap *three* together at the same time. How he did it, I'll never know! The rest of us mere mortals smacked one eraser against another—and secretly thought we did a better job.

Our suspicions were confirmed when we went back to the classroom and the sister in charge clapped our erasers together to test our work. John's sent up a telltale puff of white chalk dust that settled on her black habit!

Everything Stopped for 'Stella Dallas'

MY AUNT EL often came over to our house to help Grandma with the ironing or other housework. It always amazed me how the two of them could be gossiping away one moment, then absolutely silent the next.

It happened every time their favorite radio show, *Stella Dallas*, came on the air. Dramatic organ music opened the program and Stella set forth solving heart-rending problems. This beloved character rose head and shoulders over ordinary mortals!

Aunt El admired no one more than she did Stella. Even I, at the tender age of 11, was impressed with the insight and sterling character this woman displayed.

Once *Stella Dallas* came on, all problems of the day were set aside and complete silence was the rule in our house. Not a peep was allowed out of us kids—even the canary seemed to keep his bill buttoned!

Meanwhile, my cousin and I would sneak outside to fly our model airplanes or play our version of baseball by bouncing a Spaldeen off the front steps.

Once those 15 minutes of "mother love and sacrifice" were over, Grandma and Aunt El would have a good cry, then pick up their conversation exactly where they'd left off before their favorite radio program had begun.

When my cousin and I figured it was safe to come back inside, we'd run back upstairs, free to continue whatever noisy enterprise we'd been up to.

Our 'Toaster' Was In the Basement!

OUR KITCHEN was equipped with a toaster, but I don't remember much about it. That's because Grandpa didn't really trust modern conveniences. So we only made toast in winter…in the basement!

On toast-making mornings, Grandpa would take a whole loaf of Bond Bread downstairs and set up shop in front of the furnace.

He'd carefully open the wrapper, place four slices on a long-handled grate and start toasting in the furnace.

My cousin and I stood by, waiting expectantly. It was our job to run the finished pieces upstairs to the kitchen, where they were quickly buttered and devoured.

And if a piece happened to slip onto the basement floor? Well…let's just say we weren't likely to let such a treat go to waste!

Coal Delivery Day Held Noisy Action

ONCE A YEAR, Grandpa placed an order for our winter's supply of coal. During an especially cold winter, he might have to order more, but Grandpa had a deft touch with that old furnace, and, although the temperature in the upper bedrooms was sometimes comparable to a skating rink, the lower floor was usually pretty cozy.

A few days after Grandpa placed his order, the coal truck rumbled up in front of our house. A couple of burly delivery men shoved a chute down our basement window, then started unloading our order.

"Keep the basement door closed tight and don't open any windows!" was Grandma's stern order as the coal rattled down the chute and into the bin.

A thin layer of coal dust had settled over just about everything in the basement, and Grandma wanted to make sure that dust *stayed* in the basement.

This was fine with Grandpa, who ruled the roost in our basement. Down there, he kept all his tools neatly on shelves. "There's a place for everything—and everything has its place" was one of his favorite sayings.

I must have heard it a hundred times—usually after I'd borrowed something and failed to put it back. Now I realize how Grandpa always knew when I failed to return something of his—all he had to do was look at the layer of coal dust on his shelves!

Stoop Baseball Had One-Man Teams

STOOP BASEBALL was a simple game. You bounced a rubber ball off the steps and into the street. Chalked areas designated singles, doubles and triples. If your ball landed all the way across the street, it was a home run.

We usually played "one-on-one", but up to three kids could play. If your ball was caught in the air, you were out and the person who caught the ball took a turn bouncing it off the steps.

Our games usually went seven innings— or 'til the owner of the steps came out and shooed us away!

Shoes of Tin Made a Din

A SHOE REPAIR MAN may have been the genius who thought up this noisy little pastime. It certainly took a heavy toll on our leather shoes.

We'd stomp a tin can until the ends of the can bent upward and caught onto our shoe soles. Then we'd play tag or have a footrace, clipping and clopping as long as the cans stayed put on our shoes. Carnation Milk cans seemed to work the best, as I recall.

Inner Tube Guns Were Snappy Fun

LIVING alongside a junkyard had its advantages. For one thing, a ready supply of parts for homemade wagons, scooters and the ever-popular "inner tube pistols" were right at hand.

Uncle Clem's pile of old inner tubes was substantial, and it became our arsenal when we made "inner tube pistols". These wooden toys shot rubber bands cut from tire tubes. They were rather harmless, but a good shot would give you a sting.

A couple pieces of scrap wood and an old inner tube could entertain us for a whole afternoon.

How I Lost Van Lingle Mungo

THE BASEBALL CARD CRAZE swept through our neighborhood when I was growing up. All the boys on the block bought penny packages of Topps Bubble Gum in hopes of adding some big names to their rosters.

Lou Gehrig, Hank Greenberg, Dizzy Dean and Carl Hubbell were some of the most sought-after stars. My favorite baseball card, however, was one of the Dodger pitcher Van Lingle Mungo. It was a great day when I added his card to my collection.

To be honest, my collection was skimpy compared to the other kids'. The Davis brothers had five cream cheese boxes full!

Our cards were always dog-eared because we carried them around in our back pockets in case of possible trades. You could get three Mickey Owens for one Joe DiMaggio or two Red Rolfes for one Charlie Gehringer.

Besides trading and outright purchase, there was one other way to acquire players.

On the outside wall of a store at the corner of Lexington and Fourth Street, we played a game called "covering". It was a simple game, but it could have disastrous consequences.

One day I recall, Larry Plunkett started the game, holding his card above a certain mark on the wall. He let the card flutter down to the ground. The next player did likewise, trying to land his card on top of Larry's. If he was successful, he'd walk away with Larry's card. If not, players continued dropping them in turn.

With six players, it wasn't long before the sidewalk was covered with cards. The rule was that if any player's card fluttered down and landed on top of one of those cards, the player would win the whole lot.

Sadly, that's exactly what happened on the day Van Lingle Mungo and I parted company forever.

Spring Dip Left Telltale Burn

I SUNBURN so easily that it's always been a bane of my summers. But oddly enough, I earned my most memorable case of sunburn in early March.

It was an unusually warm day in 1939, and four of us were knocking around the Bergen Point section of town near the Eighth Street railroad bridge. The huge steam engines used to slow down as they rolled onto that bridge and we'd wave at the engineer and fireman.

We often swam under the bridge in summer, but at this time of year with the water so cold, we were forbidden to swim. "I'll go in if you will!" Monk Ryan challenged. We all agreed.

We'd hang our clothes on the rocks, take a little dip, then dry off in the sun and head home. No one would ever know.

Ordinarily I wore an old T-shirt while swimming, but the few of those "sun protectors" I had were packed away with the summer stuff in the attic. Instead, I had on a good white shirt that I wore to school…I couldn't swim in it.

"Don't worry," said Monk, "the March sun can't burn you." Unfortunately, I believed him.

Everyone else fared pretty well, but I got burned in the drying process. I was such a nice shade of crimson coming home that the guys had to sneak me into the house.

Over the next 3 days, the weather cooled considerably, and the woolen sweaters I wore made me mighty itchy for spring.

Choosing Sides Was 'Sticky' Business

A STANDARD RITUAL began every stickball game. Two "choosers" took turns selecting the best players for their respective teams.

To see who got first pick, the stick was tossed into the air by one chooser and caught one-handed by the other. They then went hand-over-hand, in turn, to the top of the stick. The last hand on top won the first selection.

The winning chooser would then evaluate the mob of players and make his first pick.

The chooser's selections were based on 10 simple criteria:(1) Can he run fast? (2) Can he catch? (3) Can he hit? (4) Does he share his candy when you shout "Dibs!"? (5) Does he refuse to share his candy? (6) Does he have a cute sister? (7) Does he refuse to let you ride his bike? (8) Does he own the ball? (9) Does he have a tough big brother? (10) Is he an usher at the local movie house?

The truth of the matter was, all of us had a long way to go before we'd end up in the major leagues. In fact, we all stank.

But some of us stank more than others. I still laugh when I recall the easy pop-up I should have caught in my back pocket, but didn't. Even the girls skating by held their noses!

Spring Tonic Was Misery by The Spoonful

AFTER WINTER every year, Grandma showed she was a confirmed believer in spring tonics…and my brothers and I believed we were in trouble.

Legend has it that the strong smell of sulfur means the devil himself is around. You wouldn't have had trouble convincing my brothers and me of that—particularly after we'd downed several heaping tablespoons of Gram's sulfur and molasses.

The taste alone was enough to make us stagger around the room gasping for breath. "It'll clean out the fuzzies and the woolies from winter," Grandma chirped as she doled out that awful liquid.

When I was in third grade, I came down with a bad case of double pneumonia. I survived that scare all right, but afterward, whenever there was the slightest hint of a sniffle, Grandma brought out the dreaded sulfur and molasses.

It had the consistency and look of liquid caramel, but the taste was nowhere close.

That was fine by Grandma!

Anything that brought tears to your eyes was strong enough to cure you. It was years before she finally relented and switched to Pinex, a much more civilized medicine.

New Comic Book Got Flashlight Look

MY COUSIN DON loved comic books as much as I did, and it seemed like we collected them all. There was Batman and Robin, Captain Marvel, Superman, Captain America, The Spirit, The Green Lantern, Submariner, The Flash, Wonder Woman and many others.

Don stayed over at our house often, and Grandpa decreed that "lights out" for us was 9 p.m. But that didn't necessarily mean we'd go to sleep right away.

If Don or I happened to have a new comic book, we'd stay up until the wee hours of the morning, quietly reading under the covers by flashlight.

Don's favorites were The Flash and Superman; I leaned more toward Captain America and The Green Lantern. I think I was more attracted to the flashy artwork than the stories. By the time I reached fifth grade, I'd gotten pretty good at mimicking the style of drawing used in comic books. That helped me at school …sort of.

On religious holidays, the nuns sometimes invited students to the blackboard to draw saints and angels. All of mine looked suspiciously like Batman or Superman—only with beards and wings!

No Time for Play on Storage Day

IN OUR ATTIC, too many mothballs weren't enough for Grandma. I found that out when it came my turn to help her on our annual "clothes storing day".

My older brothers had taken on this onerous chore before, and I'll bet they were elated to pass it on to me. Preparations began about a week beforehand when Grandma would begin gathering scarves, hats, gloves, coats, long johns and anything else worn in winter.

I can't recall what brand of mothballs Grandma preferred, but we went through boxes and boxes of them. They were sprinkled liberally in the formidable old trunks we used. Heaven help any moth caught inside once the lid was slammed down!

Invariably, the time selected for this all-day job was a Saturday when I had a stickball game or some other important activity going on. Grandma wasn't overly sympathetic.

"Too bad," she'd say. "You'll have to offer it up." That was her way of saying that Heaven now owed me for a stickball game and I'd collect when I got there.

How to Turn a Homer into an Infield Fly

IN OUR NEIGHBORHOOD, you just about had to play baseball, stickball, punchball or handball to be "one of the guys". No matter how bad you were, you had to at least try to swing, catch and throw...if at all possible, not like a girl!

When the dandelions came into bloom and grass grew thick in the vacant lots, the call of the ball field was strong.

Kids from blocks around assembled to play. The ground rules were made up at the beginning of each game (and constantly challenged throughout).

None of us could afford a new baseball, so the balls we used were well taped. Our bases were pieces of wood or cardboard held down with rocks. Deep grass in the outfield made lost balls a common occurrence.

Kite flyers were another outfield hazard, and we found them especially troublesome in March and April.

"Stick it in his ear!" or "Nice throw, Sibyl!" were some of the typical catcalls heard from the opposing team or interested bystanders.

One of the more memorable pitchers we faced was some redheaded kid from across town. He wasn't a very good pitcher, but for some reason we couldn't get hits off of him.

On the day we played the kid, Butch or Kern would slam a drive toward the outfield, but the tape would come loose in mid-flight and the ball would turn into an easy pop fly.

Eventually, we learned the redheaded kid's secret to success. He taped the baseballs himself...*loosely* so a hard-hit ball would die in mid-air. Nothing like being prepared!

Rattletrap Trolleys Were Treat to Ride

OLD-TIME STREETCARS were drafty, noisy and rocked from side to side...they were my favorite form of transportation.

I still vividly recall standing on the street and listening to that familiar clang as I waited for the streetcar to pull up to my stop. For just a nickel, you could ride all over Bayonne.

One day when I was 11, a bunch of us decided to catch a trolley up to Hudson County Park, over 30 blocks away. Someone's cousin from up there had been bragging about his baseball team, so we decided to accept the challenge.

We piled onto the "Avenue C" trolley around Fourth Street and rode it all the way out to 35th, where we jumped off. We were hiking to the ballpark when we suddenly realized that our "equipment manager" had left our bats and balls on the trolley. Oh, no!

By this time, the streetcar was merrily clanging its way toward Jersey City. We gave chase anyway, waving wildly and hollering "Stop!"

The motorman didn't see us. But after we'd trailed that trolley for a good four blocks without catching up, a policeman noticed our plight. He came to our rescue by stopping the streetcar.

Thanking him, we retrieved our equipment and walked back to the ball field ...where we were soundly beaten, 15-1.

Movie Line Was Part of the Fun

"HEY, GRANDMA, Tommy's and Mickey's mothers are letting them go to the show this afternoon. I finished my homework and cleaned the bathroom and the bedroom...can I have a quarter to go with them?"

Grandma was faced with this question on most Saturday mornings. In reality, I hadn't touched my homework, hadn't seen Tommy or Mickey in days, and had only wiped off the bathroom mirror and thrown my pajamas under my pillow.

Of course, I was using the old "crossed fingers behind the back" to prevent a lightning bolt from blasting me for shading the truth so much. I suspect Grandma knew what was going on, too...but she always gave me the quarter.

Off I'd go to stand in line outside the theater with my friends. Sometimes the line would stretch all the way down the block and around the corner, but that was okay, because standing in line was an important part of the whole movie-going experience.

There was always someone trying to sneak a kid brother past the lady in the ticket booth, claiming he was too little to have to pay. Often, little skirmishes would break out when someone tried to let his friends "buck the line".

Standing there with all that time on our hands, my friends and I swapped baseball cards and discussed pennant races. Meanwhile, other kids were shouting things like "Stop pushing!" "No butting in!" and "C'mon, open the doors!"

Despite the yelling, shoving and interminable waiting, I must have enjoyed standing in line—after all, I did it six times to see Errol Flynn in *Adventures of Robin Hood*!

Our One-Way Trip
On the Staten Island Ferry

THE CURRENT on the Kill Van Kull River ran so swiftly that you could swim a half mile downstream using only a few strokes.

The Avenue C ferryboat captain had to contend with these same tricky currents as he guided his boat into the slip. We always admired his seamanship as we waited to board his boat for the trip to Staten Island.

Captain Bunny had become friends with my grandfather back when Grandpa worked on the police force. My brothers and I were fortunate to have relatives who knew quite a few people around town.

If we ever got into mischief, someone would often say, "I know his grandfather", which sometimes lessened our punish-

ment. On one memorable ferryboat trip, our lineage didn't help us.

Bound for Staten Island, we took seats in the passenger section on the top deck. Then we noticed the life preservers up on the ceiling, held in place by wooden slats.

For some reason, we decided to put on those ancient life preservers and walk down among the cars on the main deck. At the sight of us in life jackets, the deckhands gave chase, nearly causing a panic!

When the ferry reached Staten Island, a huge deckhand escorted us off the boat and invited us not to come back. That meant one *long* walk home, across the bridge to Bayonne.

Few Finished The Great Scooter Race

BACK IN THE '30s, there wasn't much you couldn't do with an orange crate.

Grandma had some up in the attic for storing her dishes and ceramic statues. Uncle Clem kept a number of them in the garage for his tools and car parts.

But for us kids, the neatest thing you could do with an orange crate was to make it into a scooter.

Scooter building was pretty simple. I made mine one day when I found an old roller skate in a field up the block. I nailed it to a two-by-four and fastened an orange crate to the board. After adding handles for steering and tomato cans for headlights, I zipped out of our driveway.

My scooter caused a sensation in the neighborhood, and soon there were at least a dozen of these strange-looking vehicles rattling around the block.

Naturally, it wasn't long before we decided to see whose was fastest. Georgie and Don were the pre-race favorites because their scooters were made out of heavyweight crates.

My scooter, on the other hand, had steering problems and rode kind of bumpy. The best-looking scooter of all belonged to Bubba—he'd even painted an American flag on it, using bottle caps for stars. Unfortunately, though, his front wheel tended to fall off.

The big race was set for one morning about 9. My heart was hammering as I surged to the front of the pack with Bubba closing fast. But starting down Third Street hill, his wheel fell off. At that moment, things couldn't have looked better for me.

I pumped extra hard coming onto Hobart Avenue, but my steering failed me and I ran full tilt into a fire hydrant! Shortly thereafter, I inherited my brother's two-wheeler bike and the orange-crate scooter was permanently retired.

Phantom of the Strand Played Mysterious Hand

MONK RYAN, Georgie Halagowski and myself had just settled in for a pleasant Saturday afternoon at the Strand. As I recall, I was well into my second bag of Neco wafers when the Phantom Hand first struck.

Errol Flynn (as Robin Hood) had just rescued Olivia De Havilland from the sinister Sheriff of Nottingham. Our hero's and heroine's handsome visages were emblazoned against the clear blue English sky, but just as Errol leaned over to give the beautiful Olivia a kiss, a large black hand came out of nowhere to cover their faces!

As you can imagine, the whole spell of the movie was quickly broken. Amidst chuckles and snickers, the manager and several ushers ran up to the balcony. One of their flashlights zeroed in on a tall kid who was quickly led out of the theater. But 2 minutes later, the Phantom Hand struck again!

The culprit was never caught. Viewers sitting in his vicinity were either too enthralled in the movie or too amused by his antics to tattle on him. It was later rumored that one of the centers on the high school basketball team was guilty, but nothing was ever proven.

In the years since, I've watched a few dull movies and often found myself yearning for the Phantom Hand to make one more appearance...just to liven up the place.

Chowder Man Drew a 'Bucket Brigade'

THE MOST unusual vehicle I ever saw in our neighborhood was the rattletrap truck driven by the clam chowder man. Nearly every Friday morning, he'd pull around Fourth Street and onto Lexington, his truck's bell jingling a merry tune.

The truck was cleverly customized, open in back with an awning all around. The fellow who worked out of this rolling seafood shop was an older gentleman with a white apron and pleasant personality. He dispensed some of the most delicious Manhattan clam chowder imaginable...I can almost taste it now!

Every family in the neighborhood had a white enamel pot in their kitchen back then, and bearing these buckets, customers began lining up the moment the truck stopped.

The clam chowder man would fill your bucket for a quarter—and let me tell you, he didn't hold back on the clams either!

If business was particularly brisk, he'd sometimes run out of chowder. At those times, he'd ask the folks in line to wait, then he'd drive off and return with a fresh batch in no time at all.

Smiling neighbors carried the bubbling hot chowder home to their families who polished it off in good fashion.

Grandpa, whose tastes ran the gamut from pigs' knuckles to fried liver, used to rave about this Friday treat. And he wasn't alone...I don't think there was a family on our block who didn't enjoy this fabulous chowder.

Earning Pin Money Was No Picnic

I THINK IT WAS "Bubby" Allen who one day made the astute observation that we could use some extra money for movie-going, buying baseballs and boarding ferryboats without having to sneak on.

Then someone mentioned that a friend was gainfully employed setting pins at a bowling alley up on Fifth Street.

"Let's go!" said Butch Barnes.

When we got there, we found three lanes located in a church basement. After assuring the proprietor we'd do a good job, we were put to work.

The pin-boy pits were tiny, and the quarters were even more cramped because two guys worked per pit. When the bowling balls and pins began crashing around, it felt like Custer's last stand in there!

It didn't take us long to figure out a way to work in safety. We'd quickly set the pins on their marks, then scramble up and out of the pits. But no matter how fast we worked, some bowlers barely gave us enough time.

"Slow it down!" we'd shout to them when the pace got too frantic.

They'd generally respond with some nasty remark. So, we'd retaliate by setting the pins slightly off their marks (making strikes more difficult). We knew the situation had gotten out of hand when the proprietor slipped off his shoes and walked down the alley toward us.

"I painted those pin marks myself, boys," he'd begin, "and unless you need glasses, I think you can make them out! And, oh yes," he continued, "this is a house of worship, so let's watch the language."

After 2 nights of dodging pins, we agreed that the hectic life of a pinsetter wasn't for us.

Catching Crabs Took a Pinch of Skill

"WIRTH, for crying out loud! You're scaring the crabs—stop splashing!"

With those words ringing in my ears, I gripped the handle of the net tighter and eased it over and then under our catch.

"Now!" shouted one of the guys as I pulled up and secured one of the angriest Jersey blue crabs from the Kill Van Kull River.

Crabbing was right up our alley. All you needed was some strong twine, a stale kaiser roll, a net and a rock for a sinker. We crabbed off docks, sunken barges and an occasional rowboat.

Once we hauled our prize out of the water, you can be sure that we crabbers paid close attention to our catch—those claws could give you a *nasty* pinch.

I learned that firsthand. One time when I wasn't watching a crab carefully enough, I got a painfully nipped toe—right through my sneaker!

I can't recall who the "lineman" was that day, Don, Georgie or one of the Ryan brothers…but between us, we had one huge crab.

Boiled in a coffee can in the empty lot across from Brady's dock and divided among us, that granddaddy crab provided an absolutely scrumptious meal.

Supper Surprise Was History in The Making

"GRANDMA, Cliff snuck his peas back into the bowl!" snitched my brother Fritz.

Grandma's cooking was mighty good, but my appetite wasn't always up to the task at dinnertime. Despite constant warnings about snacking between meals, we boys ate penny candy at every opportunity.

Supper always began around 6 p.m.—right when I'd rather have been listening to *Jack Armstrong, The All-American Boy*. But at our house, the radio wasn't allowed on during dinner—only afterward when Grandpa liked to listen to *Amos 'n' Andy*.

On May 6, 1937, that rule was broken. Grandpa had just admonished me for taking more food than I could eat. "Your eyes are bigger than your stomach," he said. Just then, the side door burst open and Georgie Halagowski stuck his head inside.

Georgie announced excitedly that the *Hindenburg* had just crashed. "Go on!" I said. "We just saw it an hour ago when we were playing baseball." (It had passed right over my head in the outfield.)

"No kidding!" insisted Georgie. "It's on the radio if you don't believe me." So, for the first and only time, Grandpa broke his no-radio-at-supper rule. Quickly we left the table and hurried into the living room, where we learned that Georgie was telling the truth.

For us, the fiery crash of that giant airship was an almost unimaginable catastrophe. And the jolt of listening to that radio broadcast only moments after seeing the majestic craft pass overhead will remain etched in my memory forever.

Broomstick Brigade Played In the Street

OF ALL THE GAMES we played, stickball was by far the most popular.

We played with broomsticks and a Spaldeen. Because of the distance you could smack a Spaldeen, the playing field took up most of the block. I'll never forget "Yonko" Hemmelright hitting some tremendous drives that must have traveled three-quarters of the length of the block!

The action began when the pitcher threw the ball to the batter, who tried to hit it on one or two bounces. The batter was allowed one strike.

In the field, very few gloves were used, since you could safely catch the ball with your bare hands. But as safe as it was to play with a rubber ball, there *were* risks.

The most common was broken windows, especially at the corner store. Another risk had teeth! They belonged to an aggressive chow dog in a nearby yard who didn't take kindly to strangers entering his domain.

One day, Bobby Brennan put the Spaldeen dead in the center of that dog's yard. While the rest of us banged on the fence to distract the chow, Bobby dove over it, grabbed the ball and barely escaped with his life.

Sometimes we'd get up games of stickball with other neighborhoods. Before the game, each team put up 10¢ to buy a new ball. If we won, we'd often have to run home. That was because the winners got to keep the ball and sometimes there were ill feelings.

It wasn't so much we kids were sore losers back then, it was just that no one liked to lose a new ball to "a bunch of dirty rotten cheaters"!

Rockettes Topped Radio-City Trip

I CAN STILL remember when the big decision was made. We'd just finished playing a game of "ring-o-levio" when someone mentioned that *For Whom the Bell Tolls* with Ingrid Bergman and Gary Cooper was playing at Radio City Music Hall in New York.

Up till then, the farthest I'd ever gone to watch a movie was up to Jersey City and back, so I knew it wouldn't be easy to get Grandma to go along with our plan. On the other hand, Butch already had *his* parents' approval, so the rest of us could probably use that as a wedge to cajole our parents.

A long trip like this would take money, too. By this time, I was receiving an allowance of sorts, but I knew I'd need a little help from somewhere else if I hoped to go. As it turned out, my Uncle Robbie (a lawyer in New York) came to my financial rescue. With the funds he provided, I had the most money of anybody in the whole gang!

Meanwhile, my brother was successful in "softening up" Grandma to the idea. On the big day, we took the Boulevard Bus up to Jersey City…the "tubes" to New York…and the subway to Times Square. From there we walked to Radio City Music Hall.

The show was all that we'd hoped for and more. We ended up talking about it for weeks—especially the part where that long line of Rockettes came out and danced before the movie.

We Circled the Block 'Round the Clock

AROUND 4 in the morning, Lexington Avenue was hushed, dark and full of shadows. The mournful wail of a ship's foghorn out in the harbor made our darkened block even more spooky.

But it wasn't too spooky for my big brother Fritz. He was 12, and there was nothing he was afraid to tackle—like the 3 a.m.-to-4 a.m. shift on our world-record around-the-block bicycle marathon.

All America seemed caught up in the marathon craze in the late '30s. The kids on our block were no exception. Our bike marathon was run around the block, 24 hours a day for as long as the riders held out. Surprisingly, the idea won approval from our mothers.

Fritz and four older boys did most of the riding. A pup-tent "headquarters" was pitched, in which two nighttime relief riders snoozed while one contestant pedaled.

During the day, we younger kids tagged along on our bikes. Everyone else kept clear…with one exception.

The Dalys' big brown mongrel broke his backyard tether and nearly ended the marathon. Scotty Cuthbert was riding when "Bruno" came racing out and latched onto his pant leg. Scotty (made of the stuff of heroes) kept going while yelling some choice words at the dog.

When a somewhat shaken Scotty reached the tent, "Chops" and Fritz relieved him on their bikes. Armed with Louisville Sluggers for protection, they pedaled off. Fortunately, Bruno had been safely corralled, allowing the marathon to continue.

Finally, after 4 days and nights of riding, cheers greeted our heroes. We'd broken the record at last. Hurrah!

Two days later, some copycats from uptown rode around their block for 7 days. Boo!

Wake-Pulling Tugs Made Swimming Fun

SWIMMING in the Kill Van Kull River was always a refreshing delight after a stick-ball game on a scorching summer day.

There was a 30-foot trestle used for loading freighters, and some of the bravest among us would climb up and dive off. It was a tough dive because you had to clear a lower dock, so most opted to plunge off pilings.

Diving off a piling could be tricky, too, especially at low tide or when you were trying to hold up your pants with one hand.

I remember sitting on the pilings with "Chops" Hennesey, Frank McNelis, Red Kelly and "Flea" Buckley when the cry of "Rollers!" went up.

Everyone got ready to jump in and ride the huge wake being pulled by one of the hardworking "Moran" or "Tracy" tugboats.

The only boats that pulled even better wakes were the Patrol Torpedo boats that were being built at a nearby plant in Bayonne. For sheer excitement, those PT boats couldn't be topped! They'd zoom out of Newark Bay into the Kill Van Kull in formation. As they roared past in single file, we'd happily bounce around in the monster waves they made.

Penny Arcade Provided Summer Fun

DOWN ON First Street, there was an exciting part of town we called "The Stands". For the guys and me, it was a summertime magnet! On warm nights, there'd be all kinds of people crowded around looking for fun in a real carnival atmosphere.

I had to be discreet about my visits to The Stands because, in Grandma's eyes, it was a disreputable area. She threatened to "box my ears" if she ever found out I'd been there!

Whenever we went, we spent most of our time in the Penny Arcade...and my allowance never lasted long.

A variety of ravenous machines were lined up and begging for our nickels. You'd drop a coin into one and turn a crank on the side to see a flickering movie show—including everything from cowboy heroes to dancing girls.

Another favorite was the Electric Shock Machine, whose sign proudly promised, "Guaranteed to Rejuvenate Your Blood!"

I don't know how "rejuvenating" the experience was, but we did have fun!

For a dime, you could grab the handle and crank it as fast as you liked. You rested your other hand on the machine and felt a tingling electric current surging through your body. The guys and I soon discovered that if we held hands, the current would travel through each of us!

Our electrical experiments came to a screeching end (literally) one memorable evening. Monk Ryan was standing at the end of our human chain when he reached out and touched the arcade owner's sleeping cat!

We were thrown out of there for good. Worse yet, Grandma found out, and I got my ears boxed anyway!

Excursion Boat Was Challenge For Stowaways

ON SUMMER DAYS, vast crowds of happy people would gather at Brady's dock to board the excursion boats bound for Rye Beach or Rockaway Park.

My most vivid memory of the excursion boats is the day I saw a huge man waiting to board. He was standing in the middle of a crowd and all eyes were fixed on him. He was Primo Carnera, the former heavyweight boxing champion of the world! I even shook his hand!

We kids usually didn't have enough money to board one of those exciting excursion boats, but that didn't stop us from finding ways to sneak on. It usually worked like this:

We'd pool our money and send one paying passenger aboard. He'd carry a bag that had pants and shirts for everyone else.

The rest of would dive off the dock, swim to the side of the boat and get hauled aboard—if we were lucky. The unlucky ones were nabbed by the deckhands, who shooed kids off before they boarded or delivered them down the gangplank and back to the pier.

Fortunately, most paying passengers were sympathetic to kids sneaking aboard. They'd gather around swimmers climbing on, and would shield them from the deckhands. We'd quickly pull on our dry clothes and try to get lost in the crowd.

Unlike legitimate passengers, we weren't able to bring any food along. But we could usually find someone with a soft heart who would share a cucumber sandwich or piece of fruit from their picnic basket.

We'd end up having a great time at the beach—although sunburned faces were very much in evidence on the cruise back to Bayonne.

Boxball Bounces Were Baffling

WE BOYS PLAYED so many games in the old neighborhood, but the one I liked best of all was boxball.

This variation on baseball had simple rules: A box about 12 inches square was drawn on the pavement in front of home plate. If the pitcher's underhand delivery landed the ball in the box, you had to swing at it on the bounce.

No bat was involved...you swung at the rubber ball with your bare hand. You were out if the ball landed beyond the foul lines.

You can imagine the arguments that started when a pitcher claimed to hit the box, yet the batter let the ball go by without swinging. The lines of the box were drawn with soft bricks that left a mark on the ball if it landed on a line, but often even that didn't settle an argument.

I guess the reason I liked boxball so much was that speed, deception and skill were all compacted into such a small area. Unlike stickball, you didn't need a whole block to play boxball.

And, oh, the fluky bounces a skilled pitcher could put on that soft rubber ball! Bobby Brennan could make the ball practically stand still on the first bounce. My older brother Bud could make the ball bound sharply to either the right or left.

But some kid from Lord Avenue was the best of them all. He struck me out with bounces I'd never seen before. I *still* can't figure out how he did it.

'Clean Hits' Were Trouble Near Home

"NEVER ON MONDAY" could be the title of this picture, since a stickball is headed straight for a clothesline full of clean laundry.

We learned the hard way that any Monday stickball games had best be played far away from our usual "diamond" on Fourth Street.

All the two-family flats there had clotheslines that extended from the backs of the houses to poles about 30 yards away. When we played on Mondays, a fly ball would always disappear into the washlines, and that meant trouble.

It wasn't so much a matter of a dirty rubber ball smacking a snowy-white bedsheet. The real problem was the embarrassment suffered when we tried to retrieve an errant Spaldeen from a backyard with a bunch of women's undergarments on the line.

What boy in his right mind would go looking for a ball amid the flapping lingerie in a housewife's backyard? Even though Spaldeens cost a whole dime, the ball somehow faded into insignificance when you were suddenly grabbed by an indignant woman whose stare was probably lethal.

That's why we finally had to move our games down to Hobart Avenue. There, our chances of hitting into a clothesline were nil...but we lost more than one ball down a hungry storm sewer.

74

Running-Board Picnic Topped A Day at the Beach

KINDHEARTED UNCLE CLEM would never deny Grandma anything. So on those rare summer days when she announced, "Clement, I'd like to take the children to the beach!", he put everything on hold at his junkyard to take us for a wonderful day at the ocean.

We loved going to the beach, because it meant running into the surf, playing baseball, filling up on popcorn and ice cream from the refreshment stand—and, of course, enjoying one of Grandma's fabulous picnic lunches.

Grandma would load picnic baskets with enough sandwiches to feed an army and fill the thermos bottles with cold lemonade.

We kids, meanwhile, blew up beach balls and inspected our woolen bathing suits for moth holes (small ones were okay; larger ones might require patching). Add some beach blankets and a folding chair for Grandma, and we were all set to go.

But the load was often too much for one car. That meant Uncle Harold and his car were also conscripted, and then our picnic could be held between the two cars using the running boards as seats and an old army cot as our table.

The drive to New Dorp Beach on Staten Island wasn't very far. But it probably seemed much longer to the adults, who had to sit in the jam-packed cars and endure the squabbles over seating arrangements. Then, of course, came the inevitable cry: "I have to go to the bathroom!"

Thank heavens my two uncles had boundless patience. They'd join right in with the spirit of the day—and even let us bury them in the sand!

There were no radios on the beach then—only melting Popsicles, sunburned kids and lots of baloney sandwiches. It couldn't get much better than that!

Pinball Champ Dethroned!

ABOUT THE TIME Joe DiMaggio was smashing home runs in Yankee Stadium and Mayor La Guardia was reading the Sunday funnies over the radio, a new sensation hit our neighborhood.

If you had a nickel, you could go in the back room of Jerry Blanco's grocery store and play the pinball machine. If you reached a certain score, you earned a free game!

When you did, Jerry handed you a nickel, which you could pocket if you wished. That was a lot of money back then, so we played to win!

There were a few secrets to tilting the odds in your favor. Standing the legs of the machine on your feet, for example, caused the ball to roll through the scoring area just a little more slowly. And a well-timed slap on the side of the machine could make the shiny ball recoil off the scoring spring a few more times.

Of course, if the scoring bell sounded too often, Jerry knew something fishy was going on, and he'd be back in a flash to unplug the machine.

Terry McVeigh and Bobby Brennan were the two best pinball players around, and each had his own superstitions. One of them used to bless himself before putting in his nickel.

Their battle for supremacy was bigger news in our neighborhood than the American League pennant race or Hitler's activities in Europe.

At the time, Terry was undisputed champion. He lost the match when the "TILT" light flashed on at the most inopportune moment. Then, like Casey at the bat, our mighty ex-champ slunk home in defeat.

We Were Nuts for Minor-League Ball

ON SATURDAYS in the summer, my older brothers and I would sometimes watch the Jersey City Giants in an International League baseball game.

Just getting to Roosevelt Stadium out at the Jersey City mud flats was a trip and a half. The bus ride north from Fourth Street to 52nd was only 5¢.

But that nickel bus fare was a lot of money to us. I was always short for my age, so my brother Fritz made me scrunch down inside my coat as he tried to convince the bus driver that I was too young to pay. The reason for this subterfuge was that 5¢ would buy us an extra bag of peanuts at the stadium.

Once we reached the ballpark, we always sat in the bleachers. (There were too many ushers for us to sneak into the grandstand, and we certainly couldn't pay for such good seats.)

So we were content to watch from afar and listen to announcer Joe Bolton describe the game on a nearby fan's new-fangled portable radio.

We happily munched our peanuts, including the extra bag we'd "earned" by convincing the bus driver I was underage. But I never got more than a few peanuts from that sack.

Fritz kept most of them for himself, reasoning that since he'd told the lie, he'd have to suffer for it if we got caught. Therefore, he should get the most peanuts.

Somehow, his logic escaped me—as did my fair share of that sack!

September Brought Book-Covering Chores

THE FIRST WEEK of school was always exciting and a bit hectic. Neighborhood kids showed up wearing new shoes, new clothes and new haircuts, bubbling over with stories about their vacations.

Teachers learned to capitalize on all that enthusiasm as each school year began with oodles of promise. It was easy to gauge how long the good conduct lasted by the condition of the brown-paper dust jackets we had made for all of our schoolbooks.

The first week they were perfect…crisp and clean. Soon, though, drawings and chocolate smudges started to appear. After a few weeks, you'd be hard pressed to find a clean spot on any of them.

One incident I'll never forget was the time I was drawing a P-38 fighter on what I thought was my English book. Unfortunately, the book really belonged to a classmate who prided herself on neatness.

She was livid when she saw what I'd done and didn't take kindly to my suggestion that she let me finish my drawing of a Japanese Zero going down in flames underneath the P-38.

You just can't please some people.

Neighborhood Grouch Was No Art Lover

LIKE every neighborhood, we had a few old grumps who wouldn't let you into their backyards to retrieve a ball or kite that had strayed onto their property.

Somehow, though, we almost always managed to get our possessions back—either by rescuing the item ourselves or by going around to the front door and crying real tears to the lady of the house, who'd usually soften at the sight of a group of brokenhearted kids.

But there was a school poster contest every September that turned out to be a real trial for our neighborhood grumps. That's because the contest inspired a whole rash of street drawings by amateur artists.

I suppose you could say that our artwork was the forerunner of today's ugly graffiti, but ours was a lot more innocent. Since we used red bricks or white soapstone for our pencils, it cleaned off very easily.

Every kid had his own specialty. My particular "genre" was fighter pilots shooting down German and Japanese planes. I'll never forget the day I was working on a very elaborate mural of the attack on Pearl Harbor with a neighborhood kid we called "Pensi".

The two of us were completely engrossed in our creation when a shout stopped us in mid-stroke. Pensi and I jumped up and started running for our lives when we saw one of our neighborhood's grumpier men emerging from his house with a bucket, broom and an unhappy scowl. Within a few minutes, he'd completely erased our masterpiece.

Our creative juices still flowing, we decided to move our base of operations farther up the block. That's how "Custer's Last Stand" came to grace the street outside my house.

Mornings Started with a Daydream

SOMETIMES I'd wake up before breakfast and just stare out the window, thinking to myself as our neighborhood came to life. If you could have heard what was going on inside my head, it would have sounded something like this:

"Boy, listen to those foghorns on the river…Jeez, I hope Grandma doesn't find out about the ink I got on her dining room tablecloth. Darn that old fountain pen!… Hey, today is Georgie Halagowski's birthday. Hope he has a party. His mom makes great cakes…There goes the factory whistle—soon Gram will be calling, 'Buddy, Fritzie, Cliffie—oatmeal!'…I've only had bacon and eggs once this month and even then, Fritzie ate my toast!…There goes Mr. Gallagher, off to work in his car…Wonder what kind of car I'll have when I grow up—it'll have a rumble seat, you bet!… And one of those neat hood ornaments… I'd really like to play hooky today and go swimming, but Gram would catch me for sure…Gee, that new redhead from Zabreski Avenue is cute. Maybe I'll draw something and slip it into her desk before school…I wonder if she'd prefer a P-38 or a torpedo boat…"

Right about then, my morning reveries would be interrupted by the sound of Gram's voice calling up the stairs, "Buddy, Fritzie, Cliffie—oatmeal!"

Street Hockey Was One Rough Game

ROLLER SKATES and a roadway with minimal traffic were the most important ingredients for a good game of street hockey.

The rest of the equipment was improvised with materials at hand. Old boards and chicken wire made good "nets". Newspaper or magazines made passable shin guards, and a wooden shingle worked well as a puck. None of us knew a single rule used in a real hockey game, but that didn't matter—we had fun anyway.

Butch Barnes, our best athlete, excelled in street hockey. He skated fast, but the way we played, stopping, starting, holding and smacking across the legs with sticks were as important as speed.

We should have worn plenty of clothes, but we were too afraid of tearing them. Skinned shins and hands, bruised arms and legs were par for the course. Eventually, it became difficult to get enough of the gang interested enough to clamp on their skates.

The most exciting play I was ever involved in may explain that reluctance. I was flying down the street with the puck and a wide-open net in front of me.

Just as I was about to flick a quick wrist-shot into the net, I glanced around to see how clear I was and ran over a manhole cover! My buddies claimed I flew 5 feet through the air—all I remember is that my interest in street hockey cooled considerably.

Junker Joyrides Were Make-Believe Fun

THE LOT behind our house contained no swings, seesaws or slides, but to us kids, it was the best playground in the world!

It was Uncle Clem's junkyard, and amid the piles of tires, batteries and rusting fenders, he had at least a dozen junked cars. All the kids on the block loved Uncle Clem, because he'd let us "ride" in those old cars anytime we wanted. What a peach of an uncle!

I can still picture him with a cutting torch in his hand and a big White Owl cigar sticking out of the corner of his mouth as he lovingly told us kids we'd get a "boot in the can" if we ever touched his tools. We never did.

My favorite vehicles on the lot were an old Jewitt and a big red Mack truck. For hours on end, we kids would play "Al Capone" or "Dillinger", shooting cap pistols out the windows of our vehicles on thrilling "car chases".

Our 'Party Line' Wasn't Popular

ACTIVE PURSUITS like sports consumed most of our time, but we kids had a healthy interest in science and technology, too.

For instance, we learned to appreciate physics by using firecrackers to blow cans high into the air…and one time we even ventured into the communications field by constructing a three-way "party line" telephone system.

My uncle read *Popular Mechanics* and he loved anything requiring brain power to operate or build. I guess he passed this along to my cousin, Don, who was forever tinkering.

One day, Don tied some string into some old tomato soup cans, just as he'd read in an article. He left one end in his bedroom and dangled the rest of the apparatus out his second-story window.

But how would he get our "hookup" into my upstairs window, and across the backyards to Georgie Halagowski's?

Don tied a clothesline around his basketball, then attached the string and tin cans to the clothesline. Taking careful aim, he launched the whole works through Georgie's open window!

When we were all rigged up, we tried to talk to each other, but I have to admit that the phone company had nothing to worry about.

Nearly all our conversations consisted of one or more parties leaning out of windows and shouting, *"What did you say?"* at the top of their lungs. Unfortunately, this brought an end to our neighborhood party line.

As it turned out, there were too many men in the neighborhood who worked the graveyard shift. After one too many *"What did you says?"* echoed through the neighborhood, our budding telecommunications network folded by popular demand.

These Football Heroes Starred In the Street

WE CALLED IT "association football", although I'm not sure why. The game had only two variations: "one-hand tag" or "two-hand tag". It was played mostly in the streets and was filled with spirited action that stopped only when an automobile needed to pass.

Our ball had a bladder inside that slowly leaked air, so my Uncle Clem came to the rescue. He had a surgeon's touch when it came to vulcanizing patches onto football bladders. When finally the bladder couldn't hold any more patches, we pulled it out and stuffed the ball with rags.

I remember one game we played on Third Street in the fall of 1940. On the second play of the game, I'd gone out for a pass, executed a perfect buttonhook pattern and was wide open.

I was reaching out to catch Morgan Kern's end-over-end pass when an early tag sent me flying. I "caught" the ball square in the face!

That rag-filled pigskin felt like a medicine ball as it smacked me, and I had to leave the game with a bloody nose. Luckily, we'd thrown our bulky sweaters onto the sidewalk before the game, so I didn't bleed on my new "school" pullover.

It was a good thing, too, because Grandma would have been less than pleased. Still, she must have wondered why, for weeks afterward, guys made a point of coming up and asking loudly, "So, Cliff, how's your nose?"

The Joy of 'Cooking Mickeys'

MAYBE the night air sharpened our appetites…maybe we just had "hollow legs" when it came to food. Whatever the reason, the potatoes my buddies and I baked up "in the lots" each fall were truly scrumptious.

Somebody in the gang was usually eating something, whether it was Georgie Halagowski's tomato sandwich doused with mayonnaise, Butch Barnes' frozen Milky Ways or the handy apple that someone always seemed to have in his pocket.

The cool evening air of September and October brought with it our evening potato bakes in the empty lots. "Cookin' Mickeys" was a special way we satisfied a hunger worked up by a late baseball or football game.

After choosing someone to scavenge the wood, we'd build a nice fire, even though our parents would likely look askance on this. Next, we'd find sticks to hold our potatoes (conveniently smuggled from home). If no good sticks could be found, we'd just throw the potatoes into the fire.

Your first nibble of a blackened spud would burn a little bit, but with each bite, the Mickey seemed tastier and tastier.

After we'd eaten, we'd stand around till the fire died down. When it was out, we'd run in circles to blow the smoke smell off our clothes. I doubt if we ever fooled anyone.

Furnace Didn't Fight Cold Winter Nights

OUR HOUSE at 110 Lexington Avenue didn't have much in the way of insulation, so the old place had to stand up to rugged New Jersey winters without much fortification.

I shared an upstairs bedroom with my brothers, Bud and Fritz, and that room was a *long* way from our old furnace in the basement. I remember icy floors, frosted windows and puffs of breath under a dim overhead light.

When bedtime came, it was always so chilly that there was no time for dilly-dallying. We undressed, put on our pj's at top speed, then dove into bed. Being the youngest, I was stuck in the middle.

It was kind of like sleeping on a hill. If I rolled off to Fritz's side, I'd get a nudge in the ribs to get back in my territory. It was the same on Bud's side…and if my head accidentally rolled onto their pillows, watch out!

The attic door was in our bedroom. Every so often, it creaked open in the middle of the night, pushed by the wind that blew through our attic.

For some reason, this tended to occur on nights when my brothers were attending some high school athletic event and I was in bed all alone.

Even worse, that door tended to blow open after I'd recently seen a movie like *The Mummy's Curse* or just finished listening to *Inner Sanctum*. On those nights, I slept with my head completely under the covers.

Tree Trimming Took Many Hands

PUTTING UP the Christmas tree was a real time of excitement at our house.

All the boxes containing ornaments were brought down from the attic and unpacked, along with the Lionel train and all the little houses that we placed under the tree.

Uncle Clem did the sawing and fit the tree into its stand, and Aunt El was in charge of placing the ornaments.

Each of us kids had a job to do, too, and under Grandma's vigilant supervision, it was sure to be done right.

We really started getting into the spirit a few days before Christmas. By then, the radio was playing lots of holiday music and the tantalizing aroma of Grandma's mincemeat pies was filling the house.

The excitement ran all through the neighborhood, and for us kids, the big topic of conversation was speculation about the presents we were likely to get.

Between wishing for gifts, we also hoped that Mother Nature would lend a hand by unloading a huge blizzard on us. That would make terrific sledding during Christmas vacation, *and* we'd be able to pick up some "shoveling money" from the neighbors.

Yes, without a doubt, Christmas was the best time of the year.

About the Author

IN JUNE of 1944, Cliff Wirth graduated from high school and left his beloved Bayonne neighborhood to join the Army Air Corps. He was serving in the Pacific Theater when World War II came to a close.

When he returned to the States, Cliff put his many years of comic book "training" to good use by enrolling in art school in Detroit, Michigan.

He got his first job "slinging ink" as a newspaper illustrator at the old Detroit Times and later did artwork for magazines. For the past 15 years, Cliff has worked as an illustrator for the Chicago Sun-Times.

The old ink slinger and his wife, Lois, now live in Twin Lakes, Wisconsin. They have seven children and 11 grandchildren …none of whom, he reports, have ever hopped a streetcar or played a game of stickball.